THE VERMONT BEEKEEPERS ASSOCIATION

The Vermont Beekeepers Association (VBA) represents almost 2000 beekeepers who raise bees for love, honey and pollination. The VBA promotes the sale and use of Vermont honey. Honey producers are as diverse as Vermont's 246 towns, but we are unified by our enduring fascination with bees.

Vermont's beekeepers produce about 500,000 pounds of honey annually, depending upon weather conditions. Most of Vermont's beekeepers are hobbyists with fewer than 10 hives. Only a handful own more than several hundred hives and can be considered full-time.

To learn more about Vermont beekeeping, visit our web site at **www.vermontbeekeepers.org**

The Vermont Beekeepers Association is also a member of the Vermont Fresh Network, which "encourages farmers, food producers and chefs to work directly with each other to build partnerships. Building these regional connections contributes to stronger local communities and their economies."

www.vermontfresh.net

Vermont Beekeepers Association
Box 764, Burlington, VT 05402

Cooking With Honey

Honey is truly a gift of nature. It is the golden harvest of the honeybee, produced entirely from the sweet fragrant juices of summer blossoms. Honey is a natural sugar and an excellent energy source. It adds flavor and prolongs freshness in baked goods.

Honey has the ability to absorb and retain moisture which retards drying out and staleness of baked goods. Cakes and cookies made with honey develop a moist texture and stay fresh for a longer time than they would if made with granulated sugar. In busy holiday seasons, baking can be done ahead of time.

When using honey in cake baking, it is best to use recipes that have been tested with honey. Otherwise, the general rule is to reduce the liquid 1/4 cup for each cup of honey used to replace sugar. In a recipe, liquid can mean water, milk, coffee, eggs or juice. Substituting honey for the full amount of sugar may produce a heavy texture in baked goods. In recipes calling for large amounts of sugar, such as cakes or sweet breads, substituting honey for half of the sugar called for and reducing the liquid will produce a lighter product.

In a cake recipe calling for one cup of sugar, use one half cup of sugar and one half cup of honey and reduce the liquid by three tablespoons.

In some recipes the total amount of sugar can be reduced when substituting honey, because honey is sweeter than sugar. For example, in cookie recipes calling for large amounts of sugar, 3/4 cups of honey can be substituted for one cup of granulated sugar without reducing sweetness noticeably.

In breadmaking, honey can be substituted for all the sugar called for, as most bread recipes do not call for large amounts of sugar.

For leavening, best results are obtained by using directions on the baking powder can. A small amount of baking soda is needed to neutralize the acidity of honey. When honey is substituted for sugar in baked goods, add 1/4 teaspoon of baking soda for every cup of honey used. If the recipe calls for sour milk, baking soda, and honey, it is not necessary to add any extra baking soda for the honey.

Breads, cakes, and cookies made with honey will brown more readily than baked goods made with granulated sugar. It is well to reduce baking temperature about 25 degrees to prevent over-browning of honey baked goods.

For easier pouring and less waste, use a greased cup when measuring honey. Measure fat first, then the honey in the same cup. Cooking oil, melted butter, or egg white will serve the same purpose. Likewise, when measuring tablespoonful of honey, dip the spoon into oil, then fill with honey. The honey pours off readily to the last drop.

When adding honey to creamed shortening or beaten eggs, add the honey slowly, in a fine stream.

A cup of honey weighs 12 ounces; a one pound jar is a little over 1 1/4 cups of honey.

Honey caramelizes at a lower temperature than sugar, so when baking, the temperature should be reduced by 25 degrees to prevent the crust from becoming too brown.

When using a recipe that calls for eggs, add honey gradually to eggs while beating to prevent curdling.

Use cooking oil on jar and cap threads for easy removal of lid.

Most honey will eventually crystallize. Liquid honey that has turned to a solid has not spoiled. It can be changed back to a liquid by merely heating the honey in a double boiler or microwave. Never heat honey over direct heat as it may scorch and alter the flavor.

THE VERMONT BEEKEEPER'S COOKBOOK

TABLE OF CONTENTS

COOKING WITH HONEY 1

BEVERAGES

Honey Cocoa 5
Real Cool Drink 5
Honey Nightcap 5
Grog & Mulled Cider 5
Quick Eggnog 5
Holiday Eggnog 6
Honeyger 6

BREADS

Date Nut Bread 6
Blueberry Nut Quick Bread 6
Honey Whole Wheat Bread 7
Honey-Apricot Yogurt Bread 7
Rolled Cinnamon Bread 7
Honey Sticky Buns 8
Hot Cereal Bread 8
Banana Bread 8
Zucchini Bread 9
Rhubarb Bread 9

MUFFINS

Honey Bran Muffins 10
Honey Corn Muffins 10
Honey Apple Strudel Muffins 10

BREAKFAST

French Toast 11
Buttermilk Pancakes 11
Honey Nut Granola 11
Broiled Grapefruit 11
Breakfast Fruit 11

CAKES

Linzertorte 12
Carrot Cake 12
Apple Upside Down Cake 12
Pumpkin Cake 13
Honey Wacky Cake 13
Lemon Cake 13
Heavenly Honeyed Strudel 14
Fruit Cake 14
Cheese Cake 14

The recipes and information in this book were compiled by members of the Vermont Beekeepers Association, with the assistance of Richard Drutchas, then of the Vermont Agency of Agriculture. Jane Wilson volunteered the word processing service. David Ambrose and Charles Ferree contributed the information on honeybees and honey plants in Vermont. Susan Marno collected and tested numerous recipes. Facts about honey and cooking with honey were submitted by Grace Hill. Linoleum block print illustrations of bee forage plants are the work of Jane Eddy. Woodcut prints are the work of Mary Azarian. We are indebted to the Vermont beekeepers and other contributors who offered to share their recipes through this booklet.

Revised 2016

COOKIES AND BROWNIES

- Cape Cod Oatmeal Cookies 15
- Refrigerator Cookies 15
- Baklava 15
- Honey Grahams 15
- Date Filled Bars 16
- Peanut Butter Cookies 16
- Honey Fudge Brownies 16
- Old Fashioned Raisin Bars 16

FROSTING

- Cream Cheese Honey Frosting I 17
- Cream Cheese Honey Frosting II 17
- Boiled Honey Frosting 17
- Fudge Frosting with Creamed Honey 17
- Fudge Frosting 17

PIES

- Elderberry Pie 18
- Vermont Pumpkin Pie 18
- Vermont Honey Apple Pie 18
- Pecan Pie 19
- Rhubarb Pie 19
- Honey-Apple Custard Pie 19
- Yogurt-Cream Cheese Pie 19

PUDDINGS

- Cream Bavaroise 20
- Honey-Date Rice Pudding 20
- Honey Custard 20
- Honey Chocolate Mousse 20
- Butterscotch Sauce 20

FRUITS

- Rhubarb Sauce 21
- Honey Bananas 21
- Honey Applesauce 21
- Apricot Chutney 21

- Sunshine Preserves 22
- Quick Jam 22
- Crabapple Jelly 22
- Syrup for Canning 22

CONFECTIONS

- Honey Crunch Peanut Balls 23
- Honey Nougat 23
- Popcorn Balls 23
- Healthy Honey Balls 23
- Healthful Fudge 23

MEATS, POULTRY, AND FISH

- Honey Glazed Lamb Dijon 24
- Honeyed Chicken 24
- Baked Fish 24
- Honey Pork Chops 24

DRESSINGS, SAUCES, AND MARINADES

- Tasty Vinaigrette Dressing 25
- Creamy French Dressing 25
- Honey Salad Dressing 25
- Honey Marinade 25
- Honey Mint Sauce 25
- Seafood Marinade 26
- Honey Mayonnaise 26
- Blue Ribbon Meat Loaf Sauce 26
- Honey Dijon Dressing 26
- Sweet and Sour Sauce 26
- Honey Barbecue Sauce 26

CONDIMENTS

- Turnip Chutney 27
- Orange Cranberry Relish 27
- Hot Mustard 27
- Red Beet Eggs 27
- Honey Glazed Carrots 27

ICE CREAM

Honey, Yogurt, & Sour Cream Ice Cream 28
Ice Cream Topping 28

HOME REMEDIES

Comfrey Salve 28
A Remedy for Sunburn 28
Sore Throat Remedy 28
Honey Gargle 29
Remedy for Sleeplessness 29
Remedy for Hangovers 29
Instant Energy 29

HONEY FOR BEAUTY

A Cleansing Face Mask 29
Healthy Hair Lotion 29
Hand Lotion 29
Chapped Hands Lotion 29
Honey Hand Cream 30
Honey Egg Shampoo 30
Beeswax Lip Balm 30
Beeswax Cold Cream 30
Honey Cold Cream for Dry Skin 30

BEEKEEPING IN VERMONT 31

HAPPY IS HE WHO HATH THE POWER TO GATHER WISDOM FROM A FLOWER

THE VERMONT BEEKEEPER'S COOKBOOK

The Vermont Beekeeper's Cookbook

BEVERAGES

HONEY COCOA

1 quart milk
1/4 cup cocoa
1/8 tsp. salt
1/4 cup honey

Mix cocoa and salt. Blend in 1/4 cup hot milk. Mix until smooth. Add to scalded milk and stir in honey. Continue heating. Mix with rotary beater before serving. *Yield: serves five*

REAL COOL DRINK

1 sliced lemon
1 sliced orange
2 Tbsp. Honey
1 quart water

Combine ingredients and refrigerate. Serve yourself a drink but add water to container to keep it full. Repeat the process, adding honey to taste. You will be surprised at the number of drinks one lemon and one orange will make! Keeps for weeks refrigerated.

HONEY NIGHTCAP

1 glass warm milk
2 Tbsp. honey

Sleepless nights? Try this to sleep like a baby.

GROG & MULLED CIDER

1 quart apple cider
1/2 cup honey
2 lemon slices
6 whole cloves
1/3 tsp. nutmeg
4 cinnamon sticks
pad of butter

Combine ingredients in large saucepan. Simmer for 10 minutes. Serve warm with cinnamon stick.

QUICK EGGNOG

3/4 cup milk
1 large egg
1 to 1 1/2 Tbsp. honey
1/4 tsp. vanilla
nutmeg

Combine ingredients in blender or beat until smooth. Also, try blending in a ripe banana or fresh or frozen strawberries. *Yield: one serving*

THE VERMONT BEEKEEPER'S COOKBOOK

HOLIDAY EGGNOG

Beat 12 egg whites. Drizzle in 1/4 cup honey. Beat until very light:

    12 egg yolks
    2/3 cup honey
    1/4 tsp. salt

Combine with and stir until smooth:

    1 quart whipped heavy cream
    1 quart milk
    1 quart bourbon, brandy or rum

Pour into gallon jug and store in cool place for at least a week. Sprinkle with nutmeg.

HONEYGER

    1 part honey
    1 part apple cider vinegar

Add mixture to water to use as a refreshing drink or use as a salad dressing. Honeyger is an old Vermont elixir made famous by Dr. Jarvis of Barre, Vermont.

BREADS

DATE NUT BREAD

Mix together the following:

    2 1/2 cups flour
    1 tsp. cinnamon
    1/2 tsp. nutmeg
    1 1/2 tsp. baking soda
    1/2 tsp. salt

Combine in a separate bowl:

    2 beaten eggs
    2/3 cup honey
    1/4 cup cooking oil
    1 tsp. lemon rind
    2/3 cup buttermilk or yogurt

Blend the liquid and flour mixture.

Fold in:

    1 cup chopped dates
    1 cup walnuts

Preheat oven to 350 degrees. Grease one 5 x 9-inch bread pan. Pour batter into pan and bake about an hour or until done. Cool in pan ten minutes before turning out on rack to cool.

BLUEBERRY NUT QUICK BREAD

    2 eggs
    1 cup honey
    1/2 cup milk
    1/4 cup butter
    3 cups flour
    1 tsp. salt
    4 tsps. baking powder
    2 cups fresh blueberries
    1/2 cup broken walnuts

Preheat oven to 350 degrees. Beat together honey and eggs. Heat milk and butter. Add to honey and eggs. Mix to lemony color. Combine flour, salt, and baking powder. Mix well. Combine with first mixture till just blended. Toss nuts and blueberries together with a small amount of flour to keep them from sinking to the bottom of the loaf. Grease two small loaf pans. Bake 30 to 40 minutes. Yield: 2 loaves.

HONEY WHOLE WHEAT BREAD

1/4 cup oil
1 cup scalded milk
3/4 cup honey
2 tsp. salt
2 pkgs. active dry yeast
1 cup warm water
2 eggs slightly beaten
1 cup raisins or nuts (optional)
5 cups whole wheat flour
2 cups unbleached white flour

Preheat oven to 350 degrees. In a large bowl, blend the scalded milk, honey and oil. Cool to lukewarm. Add eggs; mix thoroughly. Dissolve yeast in warm water. Stir into lukewarm egg mixture. Add the white flour; mix well. Gradually add enough whole-wheat flour (around 4 cups) to make a stiff dough, reserving one cup for kneading. Let rest 30 minutes. Place dough on floured board and knead in the remaining flour. Place the dough in an oiled bowl, turning the dough to oil all surfaces. Cover the dough. Let rise until doubled in bulk. Punch down and divide into 2 loaves. Place in 9 x 5 x 3-inch oiled bread pans. Let rise to top of the pans. Bake for 45 minutes or until browned. Raisins or nuts can be worked into the first flour mixture, before you've made the stiff dough. If butter is used, add it to the scalded milk.

ROLLED CINNAMON BREAD

2 cups milk
1/4 cup butter
1/2 cup honey
2 tsps. salt
6 1/2 to 7 1/2 cups flour
1 pkt. yeast dissolved in 1/4 cup warm water
1/2 cup raisins
1/2 cup walnuts
1 Tbsp. butter
2 Tbsps. honey
1 Tbsp. cinnamon

Scald the milk, and while it cools, add the larger of the two amounts of butter and honey. When the milk is cool, add the salt and begin adding the flour one cup at a time. When the dough is stiff enough to turn out and knead, add the raisins and nuts. Knead until the dough feels elastic, but not sticky. Place the dough in a bowl, cover with a damp cloth, and set to rise in a warm place for about 1 1/2 to 2 hours, or until doubled in bulk. Punch own, and roll out to about 3/8 in chick. Cream the remainder of butter, honey and the cinnamon, and spread evenly over the dough. Roll the dough, and cut in half. Grease two bread pans and put the dough in them to rise a second time, or close off the ends and leave them free form. Make 4 or 5 diagonal slashes, on the top, and let rise until double in bulk. Brush with a beaten egg mixed with one tablespoon of honey, and bake in a 350 degree oven for 45 minutes or until done.

Yield: two loaves

HONEY-APRICOT YOGURT BREAD

2/3 cup dried apricots
1 1/4 cup plain yogurt
2/3 cup Grape Nuts
1 cup white flour
1 cup whole wheat flour
2 tsps. baking powder
1/2 tsp. baking soda
1 tsp. salt
1/2 cup brown sugar
1 beaten egg
1/4 cup oil
1/2 cup honey

Preheat oven to 350 degrees. Soak apricots, drain, then chop. Mix yogurt with cereal. Mix dry ingredients. Beat egg; add oil, honey and cereal mixture. Add flour mixture and stir just to mix. Stir in apricots. Bake in 8x4-inch loaf pan for 50 minutes. *Yield: one loaf*

HONEY STICKY BUNS

Mix together:
3/4 cup honey
1/4 cup water
1 Tbsp. cinnamon
2 Tbsps. melted butter

Chop:
1 cup walnuts

Make up the Rolled Cinnamon Bread dough. Let rise, punch down, roll out and spread the cinnamon honey butter (from bread recipe) on dough and slice into one inch pieces. In a 12-inch cast iron skillet, or two 8x8 inch cake pans put the syrup and walnuts. Place the cinnamon rolls in the pan and turn over so that they are coated with syrup and nuts. Let rise until double in bulk. Bake in a 375-degree oven until they are a deep golden color. Turn out immediately when they come out of the oven. Let them cool slightly before serving. *Yield: 10 to 12 depending on size*

HOT CEREAL BREAD

Scald two cups of milk. Pour milk into a large mixing bowl and add two cups of cracked wheat, oatmeal or leftover hot cereal. Set aside and let it cool to room temperature. Add:

1/2 cup honey
1/4 cup melted butter
2 tsps. salt
2 pkts. yeast dissolved in 1/2 cup of lukewarm water

Begin stirring in 6 or 7 cups of flour. When the dough starts to leave the sides of the bowl, turn out and knead. Keep the board well floured and knead until the dough is smooth and elastic, but not sticky. Place the dough in a clean, oiled bowl, cover, and set it in a warm place to rise. When it has doubled in bulk, punch down and shape into loaves. Place them in well-greased bread pans, cover, and let rise again. Bake in a 350-degree oven for 50 minutes or until done. Butter the tops and cool on racks. *Yield: 2 loaves*

BANANA BREAD

Mix:
1 3/4 cup flour
1 tsp. baking soda
1/2 tsp. salt
1/2 tsp. nutmeg

Cream:
1/2 cup butter
1/2 cup honey

Beat in:
2 beaten eggs
1 1/4 cups mashed ripe bananas

Combine the wet and dry ingredients. Add:
3/4 cup chopped nuts
1/4 cup finely chopped dried apricots

Preheat oven to 350 degrees. Grease a 5x9-inch loaf pan. Pour the batter into pan and bake 1 hour or until done. Cool 10 minutes before turning out onto racks to cool.

A strong hive may reach a population of 60-80 thousand bees

ZUCCHINI BREAD

1 cup dried currants or raisins
3 1/2 cups sifted flour
3/4 tsp. baking powder
1 1/2 tsp. baking soda
1 1/2 tsp. salt
1 tsp. cinnamon
4 large eggs
2 cups honey
1/2 cup peanut oil
1 tsp. vanilla
2 cups grated zucchini
1 cup chopped walnuts

Preheat oven to 350 degrees. Rinse and drain the currants or raisins. When dry, dredge in 1/2 cup of the flour. On wax paper stir together remaining flour, baking powder, soda, salt, and cinnamon. In large mixing bowl beat together eggs, honey, peanut oil and vanilla. Stir in flour mixture alternately with zucchini. Add walnuts and currant-flour mixture. Pour into greased pans. Pans should be half full.

Bake: Small size pans 45 minutes. Loaf or tube pan 55-60 minutes. Tops will be cracked. Loosen edges. Turn out immediately. Turn right side up and cool on racks.

Pan sizes:

5 3/4 x 3 1/4 x 2 1/4: yield 6 loaves
8 1/2 x 4 1/2 x 2 1/2: yield 2 loaves
9 or 10 inch tube pan: yield 2 loaves

RHUBARB BREAD

1 egg
1 cup honey
1/2 cup melted butter
1/2 cup orange or pineapple juice
1 1/2 cups finely chopped rhubarb
3/4 cup chopped nuts
2 1/2 cups flour
2 tsps. baking powder
1/2 tsp. baking soda
1/2 tsp. salt
1/4 tsp. powdered ginger

Preheat oven to 350 degrees. Beat egg, honey, butter, and juice together. Stir in rhubarb and nuts. Sift flour, baking powder, soda, salt and ginger together. Combine wet and dry ingredients. Stir just to mix. Pour batter into 2 medium greased loaf pans. Bake 35 to 40 minutes. When done, cool 10 minutes, and remove from pans.

MUFFINS

HONEY BRAN MUFFINS

1 1/2 cups sifted flour
1 cup bran
3 tsps. baking powder
1 tsp. salt
1 tsp. cinnamon
1 beaten egg
1/3 cup liquid honey
2/3 cup milk
3 1/2 Tbsps. melted butter

Preheat oven to 375 degrees. Mix dry ingredients. Combine remaining ingredients and add to dry ingredients. Stir only enough to moisten. Fill well-greased muffin tins 2/3 full. Bake 18 to 20 minutes. Optional: use one cup rolled oats in place of bran.

HONEY APPLE STRUDEL MUFFINS

Sift together:
  2 1/2 cup flour
  1 tsp. salt
  2 tsps. baking powder
  1 tsp. baking soda

Beat in a separate bowl:
  3 or 4 eggs

Add:
  4 Tbsps. oil
  1/2 cup buttermilk or 1/4 cup yogurt
  1/4 cup milk

Combine in saucepan and cook until apples are just soft:
  2 cups grated or chopped apples
  1/3 cup honey
  1 tsp. cinnamon

Preheat oven to 400 degrees. Combine wet and dry ingredients, with a few swift strokes. Carefully fold in apple-cinnamon mixture to get marbled effect. Grease muffin tins and fill each cup to the top. Bake about 20 minutes or until toothpick comes out clean.
Yield: 12 muffins

HONEY CORN MUFFINS

3/4 cup sifted flour
1 1/4 tsp. baking powder
1/3 cup cornmeal
1/4 cup diced raw apple
1/4 cup honey
1 well-beaten egg
1/3 cup milk
3 Tbsps. melted shortening

Preheat oven to 400 degrees. Sift flour once; add baking powder and salt, and sift again. Add cornmeal. Combine egg, milk, honey and shortening. Add all at once to flour-cornmeal mixture. Stir only enough to dampen all the flour. Fold in the diced apple. Bake in well-greased, 2-inch muffin pan. Bake 20 minutes or until done.
Yield: 8 to 12 muffins

BREAKFAST

FRENCH TOAST

2 eggs, slightly beaten
1/4 cup milk
1/4 cup honey
1/4 tsp. salt
bread

Honey sauce:
1 cup honey
2 Tbsp. lemon juice
2 tsp. butter

Combine first four ingredients, mix well. Dip bread in mixture and fry in butter until brown. Combine honey sauce ingredients and heat. Serve sauce over French toast.

BUTTERMILK PANCAKES

1 egg
1 cup buttermilk
2 Tbsps. cooking oil
3/4 cup flour
1 Tbsp. honey
1 tsp. baking powder
1/2 tsp. baking soda
Optional: 1/4 cup chopped pecans

Beat egg slightly. Add rest of ingredients. Beat only until just blended, leaving batter a bit lumpy. Cook as you would normally fix waffles or pancakes. Yield: 12 3-inch pancakes or 3 waffles

BROILED GRAPEFRUIT

2 grapefruits
4 Tbsps. honey

Cut grapefruits in half, remove cores. Cut around each section, loosening fruit from membrane. Spoon 1 Tbsp. honey on each half. Place on broiler rack. Broil 10 to 12 minutes, until grapefruit is brown. Yield: 4 servings

HONEY NUT GRANOLA

Mix together:

5 cups old-fashioned oatmeal (rolled oats)
1 cup unprocessed sesame seeds
1 cup wheat germ
1 cup unsweetened coconut
1 cup sunflower seeds
1 cup non-instant powdered milk
1 cup soy granules (optional)
1 cup sliced almonds
1 cup walnut pieces
1 cup cashew pieces

Combine:

1 cup corn oil
1 cup honey

Mix together in large pan. Spread mixture out on two cookie sheets. Bake 1/2 hour at 275 degrees. Reduce heat to 250 degrees and cook until light brown, stirring the mixture at 10 or 15 minute intervals to turn the mix over. After cooking add one cup of raisins.
Yield: 10 to 12 cups

BREAKFAST FRUIT

4 to 6 cups cut up fruit
1/2 cup honey
1 Tbsp. lemon juice
1 Tbsp. chopped candied ginger (optional)

Cut up a variety of fruits such as: oranges, bananas, grapes, grapefruit, berries, pears, peaches, melon, or apples. Combine honey, lemon juice and ginger and pour mixture over fruit. Refrigerate for an hour before serving.

CAKES

APPLE UPSIDE DOWN CAKE

Spread 2 cups sliced apples in bottom of buttered 8x8 inch pan.
Melt together:

4 Tbsps. butter
1/2 cup honey
2 Tbsps. milk

Spread mixture over apples.

Cream:

1/4 cup butter
3/4 cup honey
Add 2 beaten eggs.

Mix together:

1 1/4 cups flour
1 1/2 tsp. baking powder
1/4 tsp. cinnamon
1/4 tsp. nutmeg

Add to creamed mixture alternately with 1/2 cup milk.

Preheat oven to 350 degrees. Spread batter over apple mixture. Bake for about 1 hour. Turn over onto serving plate.

LINZERTORTE

1/2 cup honey
1/2 cup butter
1 3/8 cups flour
1/2 tsp. cinnamon
1/4 tsp. salt
2 eggs
1 Tbsp. cocoa powder
1 cup ground almonds
1 cup jam

Preheat oven to 350 degrees. Cream honey and butter. Add all ingredients except jam, and mix. Grease a spring form pan. Spread 2/3 of the dough in the pan. Spread the jam over the dough. Place the remaining dough in a pastry bag with a large tip and squeeze a design over the top. Bake 20 to 25 minutes till center is firm.

CARROT CAKE

1 1/4 cups oil
1 1/2 cups honey
4 eggs
3 cups white or whole wheat flour
2 tsps. baking soda
3 tsps. cinnamon
5 cups grated carrots
1 tsp. salt

Preheat oven to 350 degrees. Blend oil and honey in a large bowl. Add eggs one at a time. Add all other ingredients and blend well. Pour into 9x12 in cake pan. Bake for approximately 30 minutes.

Unlike bumblebees and wasps, the honeybee dies when it stings

LEMON CAKE

Mix and set aside:

3 cups flour
1/4 tsp. salt
1/2 tsp. baking soda
1/2 tsp. nutmeg

Separate:

6 eggs

Beat the whites until they are stiff and set aside.

Cream:

1 cup butter
1 1/2 cups honey

Add:

6 yolks
1 cup yogurt
Rind of half a lemon and orange, grated

Mix ingredients together, folding in egg whites. Preheat oven to 350 degrees. Grease a 9 inch tube pan. Pour everything into pan and bake one hour.

PUMPKIN CAKE

Mix:

1 cup cooking oil
5 beaten eggs
2 cups pumpkin
1 1/2 cups honey

Mix together then add:

3 1/2 cups flour
2 tsps. nutmeg
2 Tbsps. cinnamon
1 Tbsp. baking soda

Blend well and fold in:

1 1/2 cups raisins
1 1/2 cups chopped nuts

Preheat oven to 350 degrees. Grease a 9 inch tube pan. Pour into pan and bake for an hour and twenty minutes. Let it cool before removing from pan.

HONEY WACKY CAKE

Mix:

3 cups flour
2 tsps. baking soda
3/4 cups cocoa
2 tsps. salt

Make a well in the center and add:

3/4 cup cooking oil
1 1/2 cups honey
2 cups water
2 tsps. vanilla

Stir just enough to blend the wet and dry ingredients.

Preheat oven to 350 degrees. Grease a 9x13 inch pan. Pour mixture into pan and bake 40 minutes.

HEAVENLY HONEYED STRUDEL

The fillings:

6 medium apples
1 cup grated cheddar cheese
1/2 cup honey
1 tsp. cinnamon
dash of salt
1/2 cup chopped walnuts
rind and juice from 1 lemon
1/2 cup very fine bread crumbs

The wrapping:

1/4 lb. butter
10 strudel leaves
1/2 cup wheat germ (optional)

Preheat oven to 375 degrees. Combine all ingredients except butter, wheat germ and strudel leaves. Assemble two rolls (five leaves per roll). Brush melted butter between every two leaves. Divide the filling in half. Spread half of the filling on each roll. Start at the bottom of the dough, roll the leaves up, tucking in the sides as you go. Be careful not to break the dough leaf. Sprinkle wheat germ on top of rolls. Bake 30 to 35 minutes or until brown. Serve with ice cream or whipped cream.

During her lifetime a single bee will collect one tenth of a teaspoon of honey

FRUITCAKE

1/2 cup butter
1 1/2 cup honey
3 beaten eggs
1 cup flour
1/2 tsp. baking soda
1/4 tsp. salt
1 tsp. nutmeg
1/2 cup whiskey or brandy
1/4 cup molasses
1 lb. raisins or 1/2 raisins and 1/2 candied fruit
2 cups walnuts or pecans

Preheat oven to 300 degrees. Cream butter, honey and eggs. Measure and mix dry ingredients. Combine wet and dry ingredients, adding nuts, fruit and whiskey (fruit juice can be substituted for whiskey). Pour into well-greased loaf pan and bake for two hours. For traditional holiday fruitcake make this a few months ahead. Wrap in whiskey-soaked cheesecloth and store in airtight containers. Check periodically, moistening the cheesecloth if it begins to dry out.

CHEESE CAKE

2 lbs. cream cheese
2/3 cup honey
4 eggs
1 1/2 tsp. vanilla

Preheat oven to 350 degrees. Whip softened cream cheese until light and fluffy; add vanilla and honey, then eggs two at a time. Pour into a spring form pan. Place in hot water bath, and bake about 1 1/2 hour until set.

COOKIES AND BROWNIES

CAPE COD OATMEAL COOKIES

1 1/2 cups flour
1/2 tsp. baking soda
1 tsp. cinnamon
1/2 tsp. salt
1 egg well beaten
3/4 cup honey & 2 Tbsps. flour
1/2 cup melted butter
1 Tbsp. molasses
1/2 cup melted shortening
1/4 cup milk
1 3/4 cups oatmeal
1 cup raisins, currants, nutmeats or sunflower seeds (any combination)

Preheat oven to 350 degrees. Sift flour, baking soda, cinnamon and salt together. Stir in egg and honey-flour combination. Melt together butter, shortening and molasses. Mix all ingredients together. Cook on greased cookie sheets 12 to 14 minutes. Increase flour to 1 3/4 cups and oatmeal to 2 cups for a thicker cookie.

REFRIGERATOR COOKIES

1 cup butter
1 cup honey
2 tsps. baking soda
1/2 tsp. cinnamon
1/2 tsp. cloves
1/2 tsp. allspice
3 1/2 cups flour
1/2 cup finely chopped nuts

Preheat oven to 350 degrees. In saucepan, boil butter & honey for one minute. Cool. Sift together dry ingredients. Add honey mixture and nuts. Roll into two logs, wrap in waxed paper and refrigerate until stiff. Slice into 1/8-inch slices. Bake 8 to 10 minutes. Be careful not to overbake.

BAKLAVA

Syrup: combine the following:

2 cups honey
1 Tbsp. lemon juice
1 1/2 cups water

Heat to boiling and simmer ten minutes.

Pastry:

1 lb. melted butter
2 lbs. philo dough
1 lb. walnuts
1 tsp. cinnamon
1/4 tsp. cloves
1/4 tsp. honey

Preheat oven to 375 degrees. Combine walnuts, spices and honey. Brush baking sheet with butter. Layer 8 sheets of dough, buttering each. Spread with half of nut mixture. Layer another 8 sheets of dough. Spread with rest of nut mixture. Layer rest of dough, buttering each layer. Bake for one hour. Cool. Pour warm syrup over and serve when cool.

HONEY GRAHAMS

1/2 cup butter
1/2 cup honey
3 cups pastry or graham flour
1/2 tsp. salt
1 tsp. baking soda
1 tsp. vanilla
1/4 cup milk

Preheat oven to 350 degrees. Work just enough flour into the dough so that you can roll it. Cut into shapes and dust with cinnamon. Bake until done.

DATE FILLED BARS

Mix together in order:

1 1/2 cups oatmeal
1 1/2 cups flour
1 cup coconut or 1 cup ground walnuts
1 cup butter
1/2 tsp. baking soda
1/2 tsp. salt
1 tsp. cinnamon
1/2 tsp. nutmeg
1/2 cup honey

Filling:

1 lb. pitted, chopped dates
1 tsp. orange or lemon rind
1 Tbsp. lemon juice

Moisten to spreading consistency with water.

Preheat oven to 325 degrees. Blend well and pat half of the ingredients onto the bottom of a 9x14 inch baking pan. Spread with filling top with the remainder of oatmeal mixture. Bake for 30 minutes.

HONEY FUDGE BROWNIES

1/2 cup butter
2 1 oz. sq. unsweetened chocolate
1/2 tsp. salt
1 tsp. vanilla
1 cup honey
1/2 cup flour
1 tsp. baking powder
1 cup chopped nuts
2 well beaten eggs

Preheat oven to 325 degrees. Melt together over low heat the butter, chocolate, salt, and vanilla. Mix well. Blend in rest of ingredients. Pour into greased 9x9x2 inch pan. Bake for 35 minutes. Cool on rack 15 minutes before cutting.

PEANUT BUTTER COOKIES

Beat until soft 1/2 cup butter.
Cream in 2/3 cup honey.

Beat in:

1 egg
1 cup peanut butter
1/2 tsp. salt
1/2 tsp. soda
1/2 tsp. vanilla

Sift, measure, and add:

1 to 1 1/2 cups flour (amount depends on oiliness of peanut butter)

Preheat oven to 375 degrees. Place on greased cookie sheet. Press flat with fork. Bake 10 to 20 minutes.

OLD FASHIONED RAISIN BARS

1 cup seedless raisins
3/4 cup water
1/2 cup salad oil or shortening
3/4 cup honey
1 slightly beaten egg
1 3/4 cups sifted flour
1/4 tsp. salt
1 tsp. baking soda
1 tsp. each cinnamon, nutmeg, allspice
1/2 tsp. ground cloves
1/2 cup chopped walnuts

Preheat oven to 350 degrees. Combine raisins & water; bring to a boil. Remove from heat. Stir in salad oil. Cool to lukewarm. Stir in honey and egg. Sift together dry ingredients. Beat into raisin mixture. Stir in nuts. Pour into greased 13x9x2 inch pan. Bake 20 minutes or until done. When cool, cut into bars. Dust with confectionery sugar.

FROSTING

CREAM CHEESE HONEY FROSTING I

Mix honey and cream cheese together in proportions of 2 teaspoons of honey to 3 ounces of cream cheese.

Flavor variations:

 1/2 tsp. vanilla
 1 tsp. orange juice concentrate
 small pieces of chocolate chips

This frosting is excellent on carrot cake and any of the other "fiber" cakes, such as banana, prune or pumpkin. It's also good on chocolate spice cake and gingerbread.

CREAM CHEESE HONEY FROSTING II

 1 cup honey
 1/3 cup butter
 3/4 cup water
 10 oz. cream cheese
 2 1/2 tsp. vanilla
 5 Tbsps. cornstarch
 3/4 cup pecans

Dissolve cornstarch in 1/4 cup water. Boil honey and 1/2 cup water together. While stirring the honey mixture, slowly add the cornstarch and let cook until thick, keep stirring while cooking. Whip cream cheese and butter together with honey mixture. Spread over cake and serve. Serves 12 to 15. Pecans may be chopped and added to icing, sprinkled on top, or both.

BOILED HONEY FROSTING

Cook 1 1/2 cups honey with a pinch of salt to 238 degrees (soft ball stage). Beat two egg whites. Pour hot honey in a thin stream over beaten egg whites continuing to beat until all honey is added and frosting will stand in peaks. Spread on cake.

FUDGE FROSTING WITH CREAMED HONEY

 2 to 4 ounces unsweetened chocolate
 1/2 cup butter
 2 Tbsp. vanilla
 1 cup creamed honey

Melt chocolate and butter together, then cool. Blend together with vanilla and creamed honey. The smoothness will depend on the fineness of the crystal in the honey. For a lighter frosting whip with electric mixer.

FUDGE FROSTING

 1 cup whipping cream
 4 Tbsps. butter
 1/2 cup honey
 4 oz. unsweetened chocolate
 1 tsps. vanilla
  or 2 Tbsps. liquor

Bring cream to a boil in a heavy bottomed saucepan. Turn off and add chocolate stirring constantly until melted. Add butter, stir until melted, blend in honey and flavoring. Let cool. Whip at high speed until doubled in volume. Use immediately.

PIES

ELDERBERRY PIE

Filling:
- 2 liberal cups of fresh elderberries
- 1 Tbsp. lemon juice
- 1 cup sour cream
- 1 cup honey
- dash of salt
- 3 Tbsps. flour

Preheat oven to 400 degrees. Mix all ingredients together. Make a double crust for a 9 inch pie. Use the crust recipe for Vermont Honey Apple Pie or your own recipe. Place filling in pie plate, put on top crust and make slits. Bake for 30 minutes.

VERMONT PUMPKIN PIE

- 1 unbaked 9 inch pie shell
- 2/3 cup honey
- 1/2 tsp. salt
- 1 1/2 tsp. cinnamon
- 1/2 tsp. ground ginger
- 1/2 tsp. nutmeg
- 1/2 tsp. allspice
- 1/2 tsp. ground cloves
- 1 1/2 cups fresh cooked pumpkin
- 1 2/3 cup evaporated milk, undiluted
- 2 eggs

Refrigerate pie shell several hours. Preheat oven to 425 degrees. Combine all ingredients and beat till smooth. Pour into shell. Bake at 425 degrees for 15 minutes; reduce heat to 350 degrees and bake 35 minutes or until custard is set.

VERMONT HONEY APPLE PIE

Pastry for 9 inch double crust pie:
- 2 cups unbleached white flour
- generous 2/3 cup shortening
- 2 Tbsps. soft butter
- 1/2 tsp. salt
- cold water

Measure flour and salt; cut in shortening with pastry blender until mixture just begins to stick together and pieces are about the size of small peas. Using very cold water, drizzle slowly while constantly stirring mixture with fork. Mix will begin to form a ball. Gently form two balls with hands, handling as little as possible. Tear two 12 inch lengths of wax paper. Dust one ball at a time lightly with flour, place on wax paper and flatten with palm of hand. Roll from center to edge with highly floured rolling pin until about a 12 inch circle. Turn crust upside down on pie plate adjusting to fit and gently peel away wax paper. Fill with desired filling and top with second pie crust; seal; flute edge.

Pie filling:
- 8-9 apples, peeled and thinly sliced
- scant 1/2 cup honey
- 2 1/2 Tbsps. flour
- 1 Tbsp. cinnamon
- juice of 1/2 lemon (if apples lack tartness or flavor)
- dash nutmeg
- 1-2 Tbsps. butter

Preheat oven to 400 degrees. Combine seasonings (except lemon juice and butter). Pour lemon juice over sliced apples. Mix all together. Roll out bottom crust and line pie plate. Place filling in pie plate and dot with butter. Add top pie crust, make slits in top crust. Bake for 50 minutes.

PECAN PIE

1 cup honey
1/4 cup butter
3 eggs beaten
1 cup pecans

Blend honey and butter in a saucepan over low heat until butter is just melted. Add beaten eggs and broken pecan meats. Pour into 9-inch unbaked pie crust. Bake at 400 degrees for ten minutes. Reduce temperature to 350 degrees and bake for 30 minutes or until mixture is set.

RHUBARB PIE

4 cups chopped rhubarb
1 cup honey
2 Tbsps. cornstarch
1/2 tsp. nutmeg

Add a bit of honey to the cornstarch to make a smooth paste. Combine remainder of honey, cornstarch and rhubarb. Pour into prepared 9" pie crust, top with regular or lattice top crust. Bake at 450 degrees for 10 minutes. Reduce heat to 350 degrees and bake 30 minutes or until golden brown.

HONEY-APPLE CUSTARD PIE

One 9" pie shell, unbaked
2 cups peeled and sliced apples
1 cup yogurt
4 large eggs
3/4 cup honey
1 tsp. vanilla
1/2 tsp. cinnamon
1/4 tsp. salt
1/2 cup chopped walnuts or almonds

Spread apple slices over pie shell. Combine remaining ingredients in blender and mix. Pour over custard. Sprinkle on top chopped nuts. Bake 45 minutes or until custard is set. Cool before cutting.

YOGURT-CREAM CHEESE PIE

Crust:

2 cups crushed graham crackers
1/4 cup butter, melted with 2 Tbsps. honey
dash nutmeg

Combine ingredients and press mixture into sides and bottom of an 8" pie pan. Save 1/4 cup crumbs for topping.

Filling:

8 oz. softened cream cheese
1/2 cup yogurt
1/4 cup honey
1 1/2 tsp. vanilla
grated rind of 1/2 lemon

Combine ingredients in blender and mix. Spread into shell. Top with crumbs. Chill 2 hours before serving. Great with fresh fruit.

The worker bee only lives about six weeks during the busy summer months.

PUDDINGS

CREAM BAVAROISE

2 egg yolks
1 cup milk
1/3 cup honey
1 pinch of salt
1 Knox gelatin envelope
2-3 Tbsps. grated lemon rind
2 egg whites
1/4 cup honey
3/4 cup heavy cream
(strong coffee or another flavor could be added to taste)

Warm milk, add gelatin gradually and mix. Add egg yolks beaten with 1/3 cup honey and salt. Cook on double boiler until thick (about 10 minutes). Let it cool. Beat cream and 1/4 cup honey until stiff and add to first mixture. Beat egg whites until stiff and add to mixture. Pour into cold molds. Refrigerate 4 hours. Demold by quickly running mold under warm water and reverse onto a plate. You can also serve this directly from the mold. Yield: 4 cups

HONEY-DATE RICE PUDDING

2 cups cooked rice
1/4 cup honey
1 cup chopped dates
1 tsp. grated lemon rind
1 cup milk
2 eggs slightly beaten

Preheat oven to 350 degrees. Mix first 4 ingredients in 1 quart casserole. Combine milk and eggs. Pour over top. Set in pan of hot water. Bake 50 to 60 minutes, or until pudding is set. Yield: 4-6 servings

HONEY CUSTARD

3 eggs
1/4 to 1/3 cup honey
2 cups scalded milk
1/8 tsp. salt
nutmeg
1 tsp. vanilla, optional

Preheat oven to 325 degrees. Add salt to eggs. Beat just long enough to combine whites and yolks. Add honey to milk and combine with eggs. Pour into custard cups. Top with a pinch of nutmeg. Set custard cups in pan of hot water. Bake about 40 minutes or until knife comes out clean when inserted near the edge of custard cup.

HONEY CHOCOLATE MOUSSE

2 oz. unsweetened chocolate
1/4 cup butter
1 tsp. vanilla
1/2 cup honey
3 egg yolks
6 egg whites
1 cup heavy cream

Melt chocolate and butter. Add vanilla, honey, and yolks, stir well. Set aside. Whip cream until stiff, carefully fold chocolate mixture into whipped cream. Beat egg whites until they hold peaks. Carefully fold into chocolate cream mixture. Chill and serve.

BUTTERSCOTCH SAUCE

1/2 cup butter
1/2 cup light honey
2 eggs
1 tsp. vanilla

Melt butter in heavy bottom saucepan over low heat. Add honey, when hot pour small amount of mixture into well beaten eggs. Pour the egg mixture into saucepan. Stir constantly until it thickens. Add vanilla.

FRUITS

HONEY APPLESAUCE

4 lbs. cooking apples
1 cup honey
1/4 cup water

Wash apples. Without peeling or coring, cut them into quarters. Place them in a large saucepan. Add water, cover and cook over medium-low heat 20 minutes, or until apples are soft, stirring occasionally. Strain apples through colander. Add honey. Stir to blend. *Yield: 6 cups*

APRICOT CHUTNEY

1 lb. dried apricots
4 onions
2 cups raisins
2 Tbsps. freshly grated ginger
2 cloves garlic
2 cups cider vinegar
3 Tbsps. mustard seed (optional)
1 cup honey
cayenne pepper to taste
salt to taste

Soak apricots overnight in enough water just to cover, boil until soft. Mince raisins and garlic and chop onion. Mix all ingredients together, boil for 30 minutes, stirring constantly. Serve with any curry dish or just as a condiment.

RHUBARB SAUCE

4 cups rhubarb
1 cup honey

Before dicing, split all stalks lengthwise into half inch strips. Stack the strips and cut into half inch pieces. Add the honey and let the diced fruit soak in it for a few hours. Stir occasionally. Quickly bring the diced sweetened fruit to a simmer and let it simmer for a minute. Do not overcook. Remove from heat and cover tightly. The fruit will continue to soften in the hot syrup. For a tart sauce, reduce honey to 2/3 cup. For a richer sauce, use 2 cups rhubarb. An enameled or stainless steel pan is preferable, for best flavor. Acid foods should not be cooked in aluminum.

HONEY BANANAS

4 firm bananas
2 Tbsps. vegetable oil
1/3 cup honey
1 tsp. vinegar
cinnamon

Cut bananas crosswise in halves or thirds. Brown lightly in oil. Combine 3/4 cup water, the honey and the vinegar. Simmer 10 minutes or until thick. Pour over bananas, heat and sprinkle with cinnamon.

SUNSHINE PRESERVES

Take one part fruit (strawberries or whatever) and one part honey by weight. Mash fruit and honey. Pour into a glass or enamel dish (like a casserole dish). Set dish in a sunny window. Stir a couple of time a day until it gets to the desired consistency. Pour preserves into canning jars and seal the jars. Place jars in canner and cover with water. Bring water to boil. Turn off the heat and let it set until cool. You now have a sealed jar of Sunshine Preserves.

QUICK JAM

Boil down two quarts of fresh fruit until thick. Add 1/2 cup honey to hot mixture. Stir and pour into jars. Freeze the jam. Use as toppings for desserts, in yogurt, or on sandwiches.

CRABAPPLE JELLY

3 lbs. crabapples, washed, stemmed, and cut in half

4 cups water

Boil crabapples in water until soft, about 15 minutes. Strain juice and measure. For each cup of juice you will be adding 2/3 cup of light flavored honey (do not add honey yet). Boil 2 to 3 cups of juice at a time, depending on surface area of pan, until liquid is reduced by half. Now add the honey and cook rapidly until jelly stage or 220 degrees. Pour into sterile jelly jars and seal.

SYRUP FOR CANNING

Use 1 cup honey to 3 cups water for thin syrup.
Use 1 cup honey to 2 cups water for medium syrup.
A mild-flavored honey is needed for this purpose.
Follow usual directions for canning and freezing.

CONFECTIONS

POPCORN BALLS

Take one pint of light extracted honey; put into an iron frying pan, boil until thick, or soft ball stage. Stir in fresh popped corn, when slightly cooled but still warm form into balls.

HEALTHY HONEY BALLS

Mix together in a bowl:

    1 cup honey
    1 cup peanut butter
    1 cup non-fat dry milk

Measure:

    2 cups dry cereal (Cornflakes, Corn Checks, Cheerios)

Put cereal onto a large baking sheet and crush with a rolling pin or grind in a blender. Save out 1/4 cup and put rest into honey mixture. Roll honey mix into 1 inch balls, then roll in dry cereal. Refrigerate.

HEALTHFUL FUDGE

    1 cup honey
    1 cup peanut butter
    1 cup sifted chocolate or carob powder
    1/2 cup sesame seeds
    1 cup sunflower seeds

Heat honey and peanut butter until creamy. While hot, add rest of ingredients and stir well. Pour into greased 8 x 8 inch pan. Cool at least 2 hours before cutting.

HONEY CRUNCH PEANUT BALLS

    1 1/4 cups peanut butter
    2/3 cups oats
    1/2 cup honey
    1/2 cup shredded or flaked coconut

Combine all ingredients. Form into 3/4 inch balls. Chill and store in covered container in refrigerator.

HONEY NOUGAT

Combine in top of double boiler:

    1/4 cup dry milk
    3 Tbsps. heavy cream
    1/4 tsp. salt
    1 Tbsp. cornstarch
    1/2 cup honey
    2 egg whites

Cook over boiling water, beating with mixer until temperature reaches 187 degrees. Stir in 1/2 cup chopped nuts. Pour into 8 x 8 inch buttered pan. Cool. Cut in squares and wrap in wax paper to store. This is a soft nougat.

For a hard nougat use:

    1/4 cup dry milk
    1 Tbsp. heavy cream
    1 cup honey
    1 Tbsp. egg white
    1/4 tsp. salt

Follow same directions as above, except cook to 188 degrees.

MEATS, POULTRY, FISH

HONEY GLAZED LAMB DIJON

1 leg lamb (any size)
1/2 cup Dijon mustard
1/2 cup honey
fresh garlic
rosemary or thyme

Make 10 to 15 shallow slits in the lamb; insert slivers of garlic. Mix Dijon mustard and honey. Spread entire leg with this mixture. Sprinkle with rosemary or thyme and roast in a 325 degree oven, about 25 to 30 minutes per pound.

HONEYED CHICKEN

1 broiler-fryer, 3-4 lbs., quartered
1/2 cup honey
2 Tbsps. soy sauce
butter

Preheat oven to 350 degrees. Arrange chicken in a low baking dish. Brush with soft butter. Combine honey and soy sauce and spread over chicken. Bake about 1 1/2 hours. Remove chicken from pan, skim fat from gravy. Add any remaining honey sauce and thicken with cornstarch. Serve over chicken

BAKED FISH

1/4 lb. butter
1/4 tsp. thyme
1 bay leaf
1 Tbsp. minced onion
1 Tbsp. chopped dill or 3/4 tsp. dill seed
1 cup sour cream
1 tsp. honey
1 1/2 lb. fillet of sole or other fish

Preheat oven to 350 degrees. Grease an ovenproof dish. Mix ingredients together and pour over fish. Cover and bake for 40 minutes or until done.

HONEY PORK CHOPS

4 double pork chops
1 can sliced pineapple, 8 1/2 oz. size
1/2 cup honey
1 Tbsp. prepared mustard

Preheat oven to 350 degrees. Cut a pocket in each chop and insert 1/2 slice of pineapple. Combine honey, pineapple syrup and mustard. Spoon some over each chop. Cook for 1 1/2 hours, basting with sauce frequently. Remove chops from oven, top each with 1/2 slice of pineapple and return to oven for two minutes to heat pineapple. Heat remaining honey sauce and serve over chops.

In the north country a colony of bees will eat 60 – 80 pounds of honey during the winter months

DRESSINGS, SAUCES, AND MARINADES

TASTY VINAIGRETTE DRESSING

1 cup corn or olive oil or half of each
1/3 cup lemon juice or cider vinegar
2 Tbsps. honey
1/2 cup minced onion
1 small, crushed garlic
1/2 tsp. salt
1/4 tsp. curry powder

Blend oil, lemon juice and honey. Add minced onion, crushed garlic, salt and curry powder. Mix well. Let stand for 30 minutes before removing crushed garlic. Variations: Add crushed herbs to taste, such as tarragon, basil or dill.

CREAMY FRENCH DRESSING

In blender, put:

1 Tbsp. paprika
1 clove garlic 1/4 cup honey
1/2 cup vinegar
1 tsp. salt
1 tsp. dill
1/4 tsp. celery seed
1 egg

Slowly add one cup salad oil while blending. One tablespoon tomato paste may be added.

HONEY SALAD DRESSING

3/4 cup vegetable oil
1/4 cup vinegar
1/4 cup water
3 Tbsps. liquid honey
1 tsp. salt
1 tsp. dry mustard
1/2 tsp. paprika

Blend all ingredients together.

HONEY MARINADE

1 1/2 tsp. minced garlic
2 tsps. minced fresh ginger
2 Tbsps. toasted sesame oil
3 Tbsps honey
3 Tbsps. soy sauce or tamari
juice of one lemon

Combine all ingredients. Marinate chicken or pork up to two hours or more, if desired.

HONEY MINT SAUCE

1/2 cup water
1 Tbsp. vinegar
1 cup honey
1/4 cup chopped mint or 1 Tbsp. dried mint

Combine ingredients and cook five minutes. Good with lamb.

SEAFOOD MARINADE

1/4 cup brandy or sherry
1/4 cup soy sauce
1/4 cup Dijon mustard
1/4 cup honey
1/4 cup minced scallion
1 tsp. salt
dash of Worcestershire sauce
pepper to taste

Combine all ingredients. Marinate shrimp or scallops for one hour.

HONEY MAYONNAISE

1 egg
3 Tbsps. honey
1 tsp. salt
1 tsp. vinegar
1 tsp. mustard
1/4 tsp. pepper
1/4 tsp. paprika
1 1/2 cup salad oil
6 Tbsps. lemon juice

Put all ingredients into blender except oil. Keep blender going while adding thin stream of oil, until dressing begins to thicken. This is a good cole slaw dressing. To make a thicker mayonnaise cook mixture in top of double boiler.

BLUE RIBBON MEAT LOAF SAUCE

2 1/4 cups catsup
2 1/2 Tbsps. Worcestershire sauce
1/3 tsp. chili powder
1/2 cup vinegar
2/3 cup honey
1/4 tsp. fat

Pour sauce over meat loaf and bake.

HONEY DIJON DRESSING

3/4 cup wine vinegar
1 cup Dijon mustard
1/2 to 1/4 cup honey depending on sweetness
2 or 3 cloves garlic
1 tsp. salt
1/2 Tbsp. thyme
1 Tbsp. basil
1 Tbsp. dill weed
2 cups light oil
1/2 cup water

Combine everything except oil in blender. Blend for 15 seconds, then add the oil slowly in a thin stream. Yield: About 1 quart

SWEET AND SOUR SAUCE

5 cups chopped fresh or frozen skinned peaches or plums
1 cup pineapple juice
1/2 cup honey
1/4 cup cider vinegar
1/2 tsp. salt
1 Tbsp. tamari
2 cloves garlic

Combine everything in a saucepan. Bring to a boil and simmer for 1/2 hour or until the fruit is tender and sauce is thick.

HONEY BARBECUE SAUCE

1 onion, minced finely
1/2 cup cooking oil
1 6 oz. can tomato paste
1 cup water
1/2 cup Worcestershire sauce
1/3 cup lemon juice
1/2 cup honey
2 cloves garlic
1 Tbsp. salt
10-12 drops Tabasco sauce

Sauté onion in oil until transparent. Add remaining ingredients and simmer for an hour. Refrigerate or use immediately. Use for chicken, pork chops, spare ribs, or beef.

CONDIMENTS

TURNIP CHUTNEY

2 lbs. turnips
2 Tbsps. curry
2 tsps. dry mustard
4 cups cider vinegar
1 lb. chopped apples
1 lb. chopped onions
2 cups raisins
1/2 cup honey
2 Tbsps. salt
1/4 tsp. red pepper

Slice and peel turnip. Cook until tender in a small amount of water. Drain and mash turnip. In the bottom of a heavy kettle blend curry and mustard with a bit of vinegar to make a smooth paste. Add turnip, apples, onions, raisins, honey, salt, pepper and vinegar. Simmer until mixture thickens, about one hour. Seal in hot sterilized jars. Yield: 4 pints

ORANGE CRANBERRY RELISH

Chop 2 cups (one bag) fresh cranberries and one orange in grinder. Add 1/2 cup honey. Mix together and store in refrigerator for at least two days before serving. Stir occasionally.

HOT MUSTARD

3/4 cup cider vinegar
1 cup dry Coleman's mustard
1/2 cup honey
2 eggs
1 tsp. salt

Beat the eggs. Combine all the ingredients. Put into double boiler and stir constantly until thick. Store in sterilized jars. Mixed with yogurt, this is a great dip or condiment with crudités and Asian dishes.

RED BEET EGGS

1 can sliced beets
3/4 cup honey
1/3 cup cider vinegar
1/2 tsp. salt
6 hard cooked eggs, boiled, peeled, and cooled

Drain beet liquid into saucepan. Add honey, vinegar and salt. Place eggs in a jar, pour hot liquid over them. Place beets on top of eggs. Cover and refrigerate.

HONEY GLAZED CARROTS

1 to 1 1/2 lbs. carrots, peeled and sliced or julienned
1/4 cup honey
4 Tbsps. butter
salt to taste

Simmer carrots in water until barely tender, then drain. Combine honey and butter in a skillet, add carrots and simmer until glazed. Salt to taste.

The queen will lay up to 1500 eggs a day during the peak of the season.

ICE CREAM

HONEY, YOGURT, & SOUR CREAM ICE CREAM

4 egg yolks
1/2 cup honey
1 1/4 cup plain yogurt
1 1/4 cup sour cream
2 1/2 tsp. vanilla
4 egg whites
sprig of mint for decoration

Mix the honey and yolks with a whisk until a trail is left on the mixture when the whisk is lifted. Gently fold in yogurt, sour cream and vanilla. Turn the mixture into a thin tray and freeze until it's just starting to set around the edges. Remove and turn into a bowl. Whisk to break it up. Stiffly beat 4 egg whites and gently fold them in. Return to freezer and leave till frozen. Garnish with mint leaves. Serves 6.

ICE CREAM TOPPING

6 Tbsps. butter
2 tsps. cornstarch
1 1/2 cups honey
chopped walnuts or pecans, optional

Melt butter over low heat. Stir in cornstarch. Add honey and cook until mixture boils, stirring constantly. Serve over ice cream, topping with nuts.

HOME REMEDIES

COMFREY SALVE

Put into an enamel or stainless steel pot four cups of comfrey leaves. Barely cover the leaves with spring, well or bottled water. Bring to a boil and let simmer 30 minutes. This will make a strong tea. Strain and add to the tea an equal amount of olive oil. Return mixture to pot and simmer until all the water has evaporated. There will be no bubbles when the water is gone. Remove from heat and add enough beeswax, a chunk about the size of a half dollar, to give the mixture a salve consistency. Pour a teaspoon of salve on a plate; to give the mixture at once the amount of wax is correct, if not, add more wax. Stir and bottle while hot. The salve can be used for skin cream, lip balm or on minor cuts.

A REMEDY FOR SUNBURN

2 Tbsps. liquid honey
2 Tbsps. glycerin
2 Tbsps. lemon juice
1 Tbsp. rose water

Put all the ingredients into a glass jar, screw on lid and shake. Apply as needed.

SORE THROAT REMEDY

2 Tbsps. honey
2 Tbsps. glycerin
2 Tbsps. lemon juice

Mix together over low heat. Take a teaspoon as needed.

HONEY GARGLE

*1 pint water
handful of chopped, fresh sage leaves
1 Tbsp. honey
pinch cayenne pepper*

Pour boiling water over sage leaves. Let steep 10-15 minutes. Strain and stir in honey and cayenne pepper. Use warm, as required.

INSTANT ENERGY

For a quick pick me up try a teaspoon of honey.

REMEDY FOR SLEEPLESSNESS

*1 to 2 tsps. honey
cup warm milk*

Mix together and drink just before going to bed.

REMEDY FOR HANGOVERS

*1 tsp. honey
juice of 1 lemon
a little water*

Take as necessary.

HONEY FOR BEAUTY

A CLEANSING FACE MASK

Mix together in equal parts:

*honey
egg yolk
sour cream or fine oatmeal*

Apply liberally and leave on for 20 minutes before washing off with warm water.

HEALTHY HAIR LOTION

*4 oz. honey
2 oz. olive oil*

Mix:

Put ingredients into a bottle and shake well. Dip fingertips into mixture and massage the scalp for several minutes with mixture. Wrap the head in a warm towel and leave for twenty minutes, then wash hair as usual. Store lotion in a cool, dark place. Treatment should be repeated every three months or every six weeks for dry, lifeless hair.

HAND LOTION

*4 oz. honey
4 oz. cucumber juice
1/2 cup vodka*

Pour the cucumber juice and vodka into a bottle, seal and store in a dark place for eight days. Filter the liquor through fine muslin and stir in honey. Apply once a day.

CHAPPED HANDS LOTION

Mix together:

*1 egg white
1 tsp. glycerin
1 tsp. honey
a little cornstarch to thicken*

Massage gently into the hands until completely absorbed.

HONEY HAND CREAM

4 oz. pure lard
2 egg yolks
1 Tbsp. honey
1 Tbsp. ground almonds
few drops almond essence (optional)

Soften the lard. Add the egg yolks. Beat in the rest of the ingredients and put into a jar. Keep in a cool place. This cream is especially good massaged into work-worn hands, and for healing cracks and split cuticles.

HONEY EGG SHAMPOO

1/4 cup honey
2 Tbsps. liquid soap
2 Tbsps. water
1 Tbsp. witch hazel
1 large egg, at room temperature
1 Tbsp. wheat germ or almond oil
1 Tbsp. rosewater or cologne

Place all the ingredients in a screw top jar. Cover and shake well. Makes 2/3 cup.

BEESWAX LIP BALM

2 Tbsp. beeswax
1 Tbsp. coconut oil

Melt the ingredients over a double boiler. Pour into a container while still hot since it will harden as it cools. Makes about 1/4 cup.

BEESWAX COLD CREAM

1/3 cup beeswax
1/4 cup glycerin
1 Tbsp. liquid lecithin
1/4 cup baby oil
1/4 cup almond oil
1 Tbsp. bee pollen

Melt the beeswax over a double boiler. Add the remaining ingredients. Heat for several minutes, until well mixed. Pour into containers while still hot since it will harden as it cools. Makes about 1 1/2 cups.

HONEY COLD CREAM FOR DRY SKIN

1/4 cup honey
1/4 cup vegetable shortening
1 Tbsp. ground almonds
1 tsp. liquid lecithin
2 Tbsps. bee pollen
1 egg yolk, at room temperature
1 tsp. rosewater or cologne water

Combine all ingredients and mix well. This cream has a slightly grainy and oily texture, and in addition to being used as a cold cream, it can be used for sunburn and as a conditioner for the hands before doing outside work. Makes about 3/4 cup.

BEEKEEPING IN VERMONT

European honeybees were brought to America in the 1600s to provide honey and to pollinate a newly introduced animal forage called clover. Since then the honeybee has become an essential link in our food production chain, pollinating more than 80 commercial crops.

Vermont has long been known for its innovative beekeepers and sweet pastures. The 1868 U.S. agriculture survey showed Vermont as being, as it is now, the leading honey producing state in New England with 12,000 to 15,000 hives producing from 400,000 to 1,000,000 pounds of honey annually. Because of the types of plants that grow in Vermont's sweet soils our honey is characteristically mild flavored and light colored. But beyond flavor and color, Vermont honey is a tradition worthy of great pride and praise.

Many people, honey lovers among them, are unclear as to what honey is and how it is made. Simply stated, honey is a concentrated solution of simple sugars, mostly fructose and glucose manufactured by honeybees from the nectar of flowers. The foraging honeybee draws nectar up from the host flower's nectar glands and stores it temporarily in her honey crop. During the return flight to the hive, she adds enzymes to the nectar that begin to break down its sucrose into simpler sugars.

Once home, the field bee gives these contents to the hive bees, who store them in the cells of the colony's wax combs. At this point the unripened honey has a water content of between 50 and 75 percent, and would spoil if left as is. The honey must be protected from deterioration to be of use to a hive of bees, which may store it for months or even years before it needs it. So the bees quickly reduce the moisture to less than 18 percent by fanning their wings to circulate air throughout the hive. When the proper honey density has been reached by this process of evaporation, the bees seal the finished product in cells with a wax capping and the job is done. Honey supplies the carbohydrate (energy) portion of the bees' diet. Pollen, also collected from the flower, and stored like honey, provides the bees with protein.

It is interesting to notice in Vermont, the wants of the bee are met from early spring till late autumn. Field work for the honeybees begins in April when, if the weather cooperates, you will see them probing into the silky catkins on pussy willow bushes and swamp alders. Maple syrup producers have only recently pulled their taps from the sugar maple trees, when the bees are beginning to visit the small flower of these trees and their soft maple cousins. The first heavyish nectar flow of the spring comes with the dandelion bloom, which can yield as much as 60 pounds. Most the these spring honeys are left in the hive to fuel the rebuilding of hive populations which drop drastically over the winter. The same is true of the flow from Vermont's apple trees, though pure apple honey, in the rare year when the beekeeper can extract a little, is exquisite; it has the delicate taste and scent of the apple flowers themselves.

The early summer flow starts with black locust trees. Their drooping clusters of white flowers don't produce every year, but when they do they hum with bees, and yield a water-white honey of heavy body and mild flavor. Beehives in some locales can put in a sizable crop of honey from wild blackberry and raspberry bushes at this time, as well. It is a superior honey and, like locust, very light-colored.

The main event for many beekeepers begins in mid-June with the onset of the clover flow. For about two weeks various species of clover grown as feed for dairy cows flower and, especially in hot,

THE VERMONT BEEKEEPER'S COOKBOOK

humid days of early summer, produce tremendous quantities of nectar. Hives on platform scales have shown 12-pound gains in a single day as the bee yard hums with activity. It is the clovers and their close relatives in the legume family of plants that have turned Vermont into a land of milk and honey, and clover honey, so rich and smooth, is a special favorite.

Probably the most identifiable clover is White Dutch. Most people have seen bees working in its small, low growing flowers on their lawns or in pastures. Alsike, the queen of clovers, is a major component of good hay. Tallish, with large white heads tinged with pink, it thrives in sweet clay soils like those found in the Champlain Valley. Some beekeepers have estimated that an acre of Alsike will produce 500 pounds of honey in a good season. The nectar of red clover, the state flower, is ironically not available to honeybees. Their tongues are too short to reach the nectar at the base of the flowers. Bee breeders have actually been trying for years to develop a long-tongued honeybee that can work red clover, as bumblebees can. The frenzy of the clover flow has usually subsided in the bee yard by the Fourth of July, when the first cut of hay is down and in the barns, and by this time the better part of a hive's surplus may have been made.

Honey from the beautiful basswood tree is next. A six-to-ten day flow in early July (again, not to be depended on every year) produces a fine honey, light colored and slightly minty. The purple flowers of alfalfa, the world's most widespread forage crop, is grown on farms throughout Vermont, and can attract bees in July if conditions are right, and if farmers don't cut and bale it before it blooms. Many wild flowers, vetch, milkweed, sumac, and several mint varieties round out the summer crop and lend a bit of piquancy to it.

As summer winds down, thick stands of goldenrod and aster appear in just about every corner of the state to signal an end to the summer. This is one of a typical year's biggest flows, but because fall honey is often a bit darker and stronger flavored than earlier honeys, most beekeepers leave it in the hive. It's going to be about six months before the bees will be able to dine out in field and forest again, and each hive will need from 60 to 90 pounds of stores to get it through the winter.

So ends a chronicle of one honey season. The average honey crop in Vermont is about 50 to 60 pounds (five gallons) per hive. Many small beekeepers prefer to remove and extract parts of the crop periodically, as various special honeys appear in the hive. The larger commercial operators, who keep their bees in the heavily farmed valleys where the clovers predominate, generally remove the crop all at once and call it clover honey. Beekeepers in higher elevations often blend their honey in the same way and refer to it as "wildflower honey." It is characteristically a dark amber color and more robust tasting than the clover.

We, the members of the Vermont Beekeepers Association, one of the oldest agricultural groups in Vermont, take a great deal of pride in the honey we harvest. It has rightfully come to be known as a gourmet product. Many of the recipes in this book come from award winning entries collected over the years at our summer and winter meetings. We hope you will enjoy them and the find honey they feature as much as we do.

The Vermont Beekeepers Association

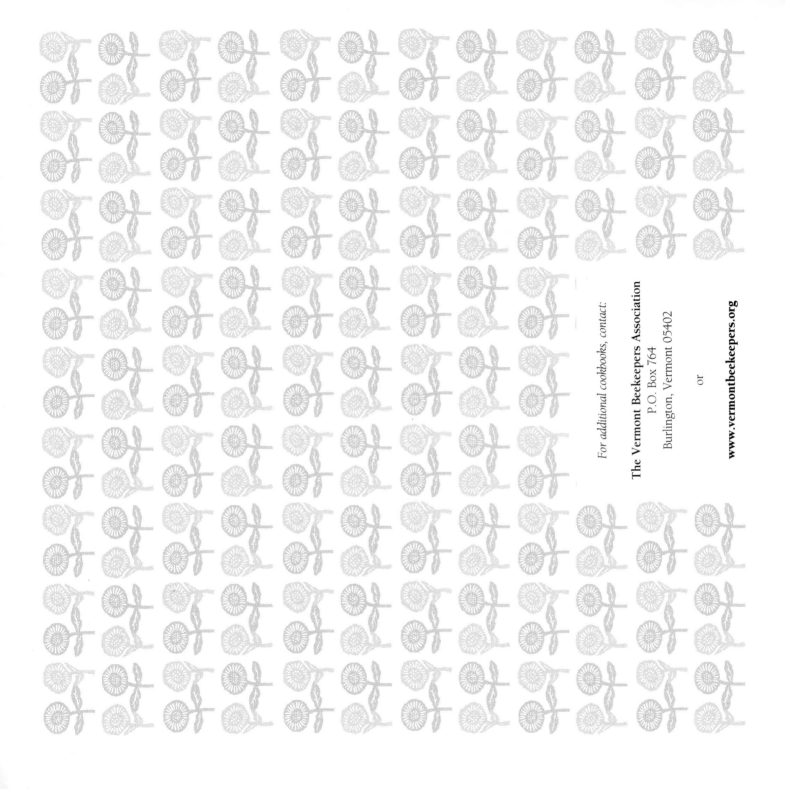

For additional cookbooks, contact:

The Vermont Beekeepers Association
P.O. Box 764
Burlington, Vermont 05402

or

www.vermontbeekeepers.org

Made in the USA
Monee, IL
26 December 2022